The Holy Mass
in Word and Picture

The Holy Mass

in Word and Picture

Original Title:
DIE HEILIGE MESSE in Wort und Bild
Third printing 1990
Vier Türme Verlag, Münsterschwarzach, Germany

First English Edition
THE HOLY MASS in WORD and PICTURE
ISBN 1-56788-005-3

Nihil Obstat:.
Val J. Peter, JCD, STD

Imprimatur:
Daniel E. Sheehan
Archbishop of Omaha

Liturgical texts with permission of the National Confer-
ence of Catholic Bishops as printed in "Celebrating of the
Eucharist" The Liturgical Press, Collegeville, MN.

Scripture texts from The New American Bible with permission of the Confraternity of Christian Doctrine.

Print: Vier Türme Verlag
Benedict Press
Münsterschwarzach, Germany

Contents

The **Holy Mass in Word and Picture** is a translation from the German book " Die heilige Messe in Wort und Bild", written by a retired pastor who prefers to remain anonymous.

It is a companion book to "The Rosary" ("Der Rosenkranz") written by the same author. The fact that both books have gone through 7 and 6 re-prints, respectively attests to their popularity in Europe.

It is our ardent hope that both these books will be as well received by the English speaking faithful.

We wish to express our sincere thanks to Sr. Cecilia Polt, O.S.B. for her tireless revisions of the translation; to Bro. Tobias Dammert, O.S.B. for his expert advice and assistance as liturgist and to Bro. Alexander Hämel, O.S.B. for his expertise in type setting and page lay-out.

The Editor

Through this little book the author makes the attempt to present to the reader the Holy Eucharist in word and picture, section by section including the four Eucharistic payers. At the same time he points out the universal content, width and breadth of this Divine mystery of the Holy Eucharist. It is the hope of the author that this presentation will awaken in the reader a new appreciation of the "Mystery of Faith."

Even children who can not yet read will, aided by the pictures and guided by their parents, happily participate in the celebration of the Holy Eucharist. Above all, however, this booklet will be a priceless aid to the shut-ins and hospitalized and enable them to participate in spirit in the most exulted celebration of the Church, the Holy Mass. Let it be of comfort to them to know that before God not only a thousand years are as a day but also a thousand miles a mere step. The greater one's devotion is the closer is one's bond with the Mystery of the Cross, irrespective of space or distance.

This book is also dedicated to all who wish to participate in the celebration of the Eucharist, but . . . It is dedicated to those who desire to lead their children or grand children to the Eucharistic Savior especially at the time of preparation for the reception of First Holy Communion.

It is further dedicated to those who search for God and whose heart is "restless until it rests in Thee my God."

It is dedicated to all who regularly attend Holy Mass and for that very reason welcome a new incentive. The words uttered by Pope St. Gregory the Great also apply to us: "Renewal will be the daily task of everyone of us confronted as we are with the lassitude and indifference of our fallen nature. There is no level of perfection which will not call for still greater excellence."

St. Paul writes:

"I am speaking the truth, I am not lying: my conscience bears me witness in the Holy Spirit, that I have great sorrow and unceasing anguish in my heart on account of my brothers and countrymen for to this day a veil covers their hearts as soon as Moses is read."

(Rom 9, 1ff)

This "anguish" is graphically expressed in a carving called the "Synagogue" in the cathedral in Strassburg. Head bowed down, eyes blindfolded, a broken staff in hand . . .

Dear Apostle Paul:

Also many Christians wear a blindfold over their eyes and hearts. We, too, have reason for 'great sorrow and unceasing anguish in our hearts.' So many of our brothers and sisters do not appreciate the most precious legacy the Son of God has given us in the holy Sacrifice of the Mass.

Our picture shows the Church as the bride of the heavenly Spouse directing her questioning gaze upon us. Do we sufficiently appreciate the Eucharist, through which we continually receive the fruits of the holy sacrifice until the second coming? The cross and the chalice remind us of it.

In the words of Pope John Paul II:

"We should ever more diligently endeavor to immerse ourselves more deeply into and try to comprehend more thoroughly the legacy the Son of God has bequeathed to us in his sacrifice on the cross. For it is 'grace to clearly become conscious of the fact that the sacrifice of the cross is present to us in every eucharistic celebration and that the faithful receive the fruits of it as their daily food and thus become cognizant of its continuous effect in their life.'"

Our picture:
The woman looking for the lost coin (cf. Lk 15,8). The Eucharist is worth more than all the gold in the world.

"Nevertheless the liturgy is the summit toward which the activity of the Church is directed; at the same time it is the fountain from which all her power flows."

Partaking in the celebration of the Liturgy here on earth is a foretaste of that heavenly Liturgy which is celebrated in the holy city of Jerusalem. We journey toward this celebration as pilgrims."

(from Constitution on Sacred Liturgy).

Our picture: Our Heavenly Father and the Lamb of God who has shed his blood for us.

Paul and Barnabas assembled the congregation and reported what great things the Lord had worked through them and that he opened the door of faith to the heathens.

(Acts 14,2)

Jesus opens the door of his innermost sanctuary to all who participate in faith at the Holy Eucharist. According to the degree of their devotion, they will receive the fruits of the Holy Sacrifice for themselves as well as for others, for the living and the departed. It is not only through Paul and Barnabas, but also through you, that the Lord makes available the most precious treasure of our world, the Holy Mass.

The Holy Mass

Liturgy of the Word

The Entrance Antiphon

21

Blessed be God the Father and his only-begotten Son and the Holy Spirit:
For he has shown that he loves us.

In the name of the Father, and of the Son, and of the Holy Spirit. Amen
The grace of our Lord Jesus Christ and the love of God and the fellowship of the Holy Spirit be with you all.

"The more the Holy Trinity is glorified, the dignity of the human being becomes more evident."

(Pope John Paul II)

I confess to almighty God, and to you my brothers and sisters, that I have sinned through my own fault in my thoughts and in my words, in what I have done, and in what I have failed to do;

The confession of faults and return of the prodigal son:
"Father, I have sinned before you and heaven. I am no longer worthy to be called your child . . . "

and I ask blessed Mary, ever virgin, all the angels and saints, and you, my brothers and sisters, to pray for me to the Lord our God.

May almighty God have mercy on us, forgive us our sins, and bring us to everlasting life. Amen

Christ is the sole mediator. This does not exclude the mediation of the saints.

Lord, have mercy.
Lord, have mercy.
Christ, have mercy.
Christ, have mercy.
Lord, have mercy.
Lord, have mercy.

We can not express our total dependence
on God in a more childlike and profound
invocation than this. Everything depends
upon God. We, by ourselves, are nothing.

Gloria

Glory to God in the highest, and peace to his people on earth. Lord God, heavenly King, almighty God and Father,

My soul rejoices in the exalted majesty of my God. Where is the human tongue that is worthy to call you God? This is why I call to heaven for assistance.

(St. Basil the Great)

30

we worship you,

We, too, want to join the choirs of angels.
How inadequate is our speech when we
desire to speak of you, or to you.
Yet woe to those who keep silent
about you!
Greater woe to those who blaspheme you.

(cf. St. Augustine)

we give you thanks,
we praise you for your glory.
Lord Jesus Christ,
only Son of the Father,

Praise the Lord in his sanctuary, praise him
in the firmament of his strength.
Praise him for his mighty deeds, praise him
for his sovereign majesty.
Praise him with the blast of the trumpet,
praise him with lyre and harp.
Praise him with timbrel and dance, praise
him with strings and pipe.
Let everything that has breath praise the
Lord.

(Ps. 150, 1-6)

**Lord God,
Lamb of God,
you take away the sin
of the world:
have mercy on us;**

The Good Shepherd:
Why would you go so far on account of one
lost sheep?
You went even further: You yourself became the Lamb, the sacrificial lamb, that
takes away the sin of the world.

**you are seated at the right hand
of the Father:
receive our prayer.**

Sin is the most heinous thing there is, the
filthiest quagmire, the most ghastly abyss.
Only one can save us, God! He has come to
deliver us! But at what price!

For you alone are the Holy One,
you alone are the Lord,
you alone are the Most High,
Jesus Christ,
with the Holy Spirit,
in the glory of God the Father.
Amen.

Great God of my life!
I will praise you from sea to sea and from
one end of the earth to the other.
With a song on my lips I will immerse myself in the ocean of your glory.

Let us pray:

Heavenly Father, we have assembled here in the name of your Son. He is in our midst. Let us join in the sacrifice of praise which He offers you and make us worthy of this happy service.

The more recollected you are,
the closer you are to God.
The more you identify yourself with the holy sacrifice,
the richer will be your reward.

We ask this through our Lord Jesus Christ, your Son, who lives and reigns with you and the Holy Spirit, one God for ever and ever. Amen.

We direct our petitions to the Father through Jesus Christ because Jesus has the most holy and intimate relationship with the Father as well as with the whole Church.

A reading from the Prophet Ezekiel

Thus says the Lord: But if the wicked man turns away from all the sins he committed, if he keeps all my statues and does what is right and just he shall surely live, he shall not die.

(Ez. 18,21).

In the responsorial psalm (or song) we pray that the word of God may become ever more efficacious for us.

Responsorial Psalm

If today you hear his voice, harden not your hearts.

Come, let us bow down in worship; let us kneel before the Lord who made us. For he is our God, and we are the people he shepherds, the flock he guides.
Oh, that today you hear his voice "Harden not your hearts as at Meribah, as in the day of Massah in the desert, where your fathers tempted me."

(fr. Ps. 95).

After leaving the church the word of God should not dissipate like a fog.

A reading from a letter of Paul to the Romans:

O the depth of the riches and wisdom and knowledge of God! How inscrutable are his judgments and how unsearchable his ways! "For who has known the mind of the Lord or who has been his counselor?"
"Or who has given him anything that he may be repaid?"
For from him and through him and for him are all things.
To him be glory forever. Amen.

(Rom. 11, 33-36)

Alleluia.

Glory to the Father,
the Son,
and the Holy Spirit,
to God who is,
who was,
and who is to come.

Alleluia,   All

uia,   Alleluia

The Gospel

**The Lord be with you.
And also with you.
A reading from the holy gospel
according to John.**

Glory to you, Lord.

The Church steadfastly believes that the
four Evangelists Matthew, Mark, Luke and
John handed down the historical character
of Christ and his teachings in a reliable
way.

Jesus said: "Whoever eats my flesh and drinks my blood has eternal life, and I will raise him on the last day."

(John 6, 54)

Then many of the disciples who were listening said, "This saying is hard; who can accept it?"

(John 6, 60)

Indeed this saying is hard unless it is accepted in childlike simplicity, with the trust of a friend and with the surrender of unquestioning love.

The homily:

The word of man –
and yet the word of God!
For Jesus said:
"Whoever hears you,
hears me!"

Be convinced that God accepts your word
of prayer in the same measure as you accept
his word in the homily.

(St. Francis de Sales, Philothea 2, 17)

62

Today, when you hear the word of God, harden not your heart!

I ask myself:
Do I want to hear God's word in the sermon, or am I like a person ready to cast stones; or like the Pharisee who wants to critique and challenge the word of God?

Whoever is of God,
hears God's word.

I remember the deeds of the Lord;
yes, I remember your wonders of old.
And I meditate on your works;
your exploits I ponder, O God,
your way is holy;
what great God is there like our God?
You are the God who works wonders;
among the people you have made known
your power.

(Ps 77, 12-15)

When he comes home to his own he will tell them the wonders the Lord has done and the mercy he has shown.

Our picture:
Sts. Ann and Joachim instruct Mary, their daughter, in Holy Scripture. All families should likewise ponder and discuss the word of God.

Parents who act thus are messengers of God's joy, as was the angel at the annunciation: "Annuncio vobis", – "I announce to you" a great joy for all the nations, the joy of the coming of the Savior in the form of the flesh.

At the holy sacrifice of the Mass, Jesus comes anew in the form of bread and wine. What joy! The shepherds passed on the good news. Let us, too, pass it on.

The profession of faith:

We believe in one God, the Father, the Almighty, maker of heaven and earth,

There is no human being who has not been chosen by Christ and the Holy Spirit to glorify the Father! Our countenance should radiate the glory of God.

72

of all that is seen
and unseen.

With incomprehensible and unspeakable power the Lord, our God, raised to the threshold of existence that which did not exist.

(St. Cyril of Alexandria)

We believe in one Lord, Jesus Christ, the only Son of God, eternally begotten of the Father.

No one has ever seen God. Solely, the Only-begotten, who rests on the bosom of the Father, has told us about the most intimate mystery of God. We participate in this mystery as brothers and sisters of Christ.

God from God,
Light from Light,
true God from true God,
begotten, not made,
one in Being with the Father.
Through him all things
were made.

The sanctuary light burning before the tabernacle is a gentle, but insistent reminder that Jesus is here present for us. He is the light in our darkest and hardest hours, for he is the true light that illumines the world.

For us men and for our salvation he came down from heaven:

Jesus descended from his heavenly glory to our earthly wretchedness. After witnessing the birth of the Son of God nothing about God need surprise us.

by the power of the Holy Spirit he was born of the Virgin Mary, and became man.

The mind and heart of the Church turns to the Holy Spirit at the end of the 20th century with a view to the up-coming third millennium since the appearance of Jesus Christ who was conceived by the Holy Spirit.

For our sake he was crucified under Pontius Pilate;

This is the strongest proof of the love God has for us! For us, for you and me, He descended to earth, even under the earth, He, who is enthroned on high.

he suffered, died,
and was buried.

The Christian religion began in a grave.
Since Christ has lain in the grave, all Christian graves are hallowed.

On the third day he rose again in fulfillment of the Scriptures; he ascended into heaven and is seated at the right hand of the Father.

His resurrection, ascension, and being seated at the right hand of the Father as our intercessor are the greatest sureties of our future.

He will come again in glory to judge the living and the dead, and his kingdom will have no end.

Of Christ alone can it be said:
His reign will have no end. His judgment alone counts. His throne stands for all time. May he open the portals of heaven for us.

We believe in the Holy Spirit, the Lord, the giver of life, who proceeds from the Father and the Son.
With the Father and the Son he is worshipped and glorified.
He has spoken through the Prophets.

The Holy Spirit is unceasingly operative in the Church to instruct her in all truths.
The Holy Spirit is also active in deepening our relationship with the Father and the Son.

We believe in one holy catholic and apostolic Church.

Christ bestows these four attributes upon his Church: the One, Holy, Catholic, and Apostolic. Because of these characteristics, the Church differs from all other organizations, religions and denominations.

Whoever has eyes recognizes in her the mark of God for humankind.

We acknowledge one baptism for the forgiveness of sins.
We look for the resurrection of the dead, and the life of the world to come. Amen.

At baptism we are figuratively immersed into the life of the triune God. Thus, we may go forward and immerse ourselves deeper into eternal life in Him who preceded us by dying for us.

Let us pray:

Jesus Christ, you prayed for Peter that his faith should not falter. Strengthen our faith.
You heard the prayer of the first Christians. Increase our trust.
You healed many sick. Grant us ardent love.
Your mercy endures from generation to generation. Amen

The Early Church gives us an example of constant and trustful intercessory prayer:
While Peter was in prison the congregation prayed unceasingly to God . . .
And God sent an angel to rescue him.

Liturgy
of the Eucharist

Preparation of Gifts

Blessed are you, Lord, God of all creation. Through your goodness we have this bread to offer, which earth has given and human hands have made. It will become for us the bread of life.

(Blessed be God for ever.)

I know, that what I bring to you is little, for to you I owe everything. I thank you Lord that I may respond to your love in a small measure.

By the mystery of this water and wine may we come to share in the divinity of Christ, who humbled himself to share in our humanity.

We, as children of God, may direct such bold petitions to our Heavenly Father.

Blessed are you, Lord, God of all creation. Through your goodness we have this wine to offer, fruit of the vine and work of human hands. It will become our spiritual drink.

(Blessed be God for ever.)

Never permit us to take your gifts for granted!
Give us the grace to pray for them daily, and to give you thanks, joy-filled thanks!

Lord God, we ask you to receive us and be pleased with the sacrifice we offer you with humble and contrite hearts.

Both, the bread of life and the chalice of salvation, have eternal consequences! The Prophets already searched for this salvation. They foretold the grace that was to be ours.

Lord, wash away my iniquity; cleanse me from my sin.

Our dual picture:

Left: Peter warms himself at the camp fire and denies our Lord.

Right: The cock's crow reminds Peter of Jesus' prophesy. He recognizes his guilt and repents it bitterly.

110

periens os suum;

Nonecanta
Domeccet

br hodie
me negab

an cilla

mo non audiens
uo redar guittones

United with Christ's sacrifice our prayer rises like incense to our heavenly Father.

For you are a chosen race, a royal priesthood, a holy people, so you may announce and spread the great deeds of the Lord who has called you from darkness into his wonderful light.

Pray, brethren, that our sacrifice may be acceptable to God, the almighty Father.

May the Lord accept the sacrifice at your hands for the praise and glory of his name, for our good, and the good of all his church.

The Eucharist radiates throughout the world, for it is fed by Christ's sacrifice on the cross.

Prayer over the Gifts

Father, receive these gifts which our Lord Jesus Christ has asked us to offer in his memory.
May our obedient service bring us to the fullness of your redemption.
We ask this in the name of Jesus the Lord. Amen.

Our picture:
Moses was a man of action, but also a man of intensive and intercessory prayer.

The "Eucharistic Prayer" is highlight of each Mass.

The mystic Christ, that is: Christ, the head, with members of his body, with the Pilgrim, the Suffering and Triumphant Church becomes active as priest of the sacrifice and at the same time sacrificial gift to the heavenly Father.

Eucharistic Prayer II

The Lord be with you.
And also with you.
Lift up your hearts.
We lift them up to the Lord.

Let us give thanks to the Lord
our God.
It is right to give him thanks and
praise.

The churches and their steeples of former
faith-filled centuries reached for the skies,
thus should our hearts be raised to God in
prayer and thanksgiving.

Preface

Father, it is our duty and our salvation, always and everywhere to give you thanks through your beloved Son, Jesus Christ. He is the Word through whom you made the universe,

Always and everywhere we should give you thanks. Did not Jesus thank the Father for the expectation of his death? And what a death! He gave his life and shed his blood for us.

122

the Savior you sent to redeem us. By the power of the Holy Spirit he took flesh and was born of the Virgin Mary.

The almighty God has become a compassionate human being. Of what should we be afraid? Now, in heaven, he is filled with the same love and goodness as he had while on earth.

For our sake he opened his arms on the cross;

Our liturgical celebration of the Eucharist must not defame its character of atonement (expiation), nor the fact that the glorified Lord is now present upon the altar.

he put an end to death
and revealed the resurrection.
In this he fulfilled your will
and won for you a holy people.

For if you confess with your lips that Jesus
is Lord and believe in your heart that God
raised him from the dead, you will be
saved."

(Rom. 10, 9)

And so we join the angels and the saints in proclaiming your glory as we sing (say):

We praise Our Heavenly Father together with the Triumphant Church (the angels and saints in heaven), with the Pilgrim Church on earth and with the Suffering Church in Purgatory.

Holy, holy, holy
Lord, God of power and might,

We could not be so bold as to come before the thrice holy God and pronounce his name if he had not called us to share in his holiness.

Heaven and earth
are full of your glory.
Hosanna in the highest.

"From the greatness and the beauty of
created things their prodigal author is
seen."
. . . for the original source of beauty fashioned them."

(Wis. 13, 5 and 3)

Blessed is he who comes in the name of the Lord.
Hosanna in the highest.

Redeemer of the world!
How humble was your first coming!
How humble your entry into Jerusalem!
Humbler still is your coming in the Eucharist!
How majestic will be your final coming!

Lord, you are holy indeed, the fountain of all holiness.

The sacrifice of the Mass is, from first to last, the work of the triune God.
It is our task to open ourselves to the stream of grace and to a willing participation. "The fountainhead of the Church is the Father, the Son and the Holy Spirit."

Let your Spirit come upon these gifts to make them holy,
so that they may become for us the body and blood of our Lord, Jesus Christ.

Jesus was born for us through the Holy Spirit. He now becomes present to us through the Holy Spirit.

Before he was given up to death, a death he freely accepted, he took bread and gave you thanks. He broke the bread, gave it to his disciples, and said:

Take this, all of you, and eat it: this is my body which will be given up for you.

"Do you believe you are still among humans and remain on earth? Or are you not rather transported to heaven."

(St. John Chrysostom)

When supper was ended, he took the cup. Again he gave you thanks and praise, gave the cup to his disciples, and said:
Take this, all of you, and drink from it:
this is the cup of my blood, the blood of the new and everlasting covenant. It will be shed for you and for all so that sins may be forgiven.

When Jesus offered the last drop of his blood upon Golgotha he had already placed that same love into the cup at the last supper for our salvation. He continues to do so until His second coming.

Do this in memory of me.

The Apostles passed on to their successors the powers they had received from Jesus. Paul writes to Timothy whom he had appointed bishop of Ephesus: "For this reason, I remind you to stir into flame the gift of God that you have through the imposition of my hands." (1 Tim. 6).

He also admonishes him: "Do not lay hands too readily on anyone, and do not share in another's sins. Keep yourself pure." (1 Tim. 22).

146

Let us proclaim the mystery
of faith:

Dying you destroyed our death,

By the sacrifice of the Eucharist Jesus re-
moves all barriers of time and space. De-
pending on our interior disposition we can,
like Mary, John, or Mary Magdalene stand
close by the cross, or we can be indifferent
spectators from across the street.

rising you restored our life.
Lord Jesus, come in glory.

"To the King of ages, immortal, invisible,
the only God, be honor and glory for ever
and ever. Amen."

(1 Tim. 1, 17)

In memory of his death and resurrection, we offer you, Father, this life-giving bread, this saving cup.

Do not be fearful of my golden chalice! Do not be frightened by the glow of my candles. They are but tender hands stretched out over my mystery.

153

We thank you for counting us worthy to stand in your presence and serve you.
May all of us who share in the body and blood of Christ be brought together in unity by the Holy Spirit.

Would it not be good if I, like the statesman Thomas More, the laborer Matt Talbot and the millionaire Lo Pa Hong, attended Holy Mass and received Holy Communion more frequently, even daily?

Lord, remember your Church
throughout the world;
make us grow in love,

They lived their love

St. Maximilian Kolbe
1894–1941

Bl. Fr. Rupert Mayer, S.J.
1876–1945

St. Peter Claver
1580–1654

Lo Pa Hong, Shanghai
1874–1937

S. PETRUS C
☩ S. SEP

together with

Peter, the first Pope

(N), our Pope

and his present successor

N. our bishop,

Let us pray for our bishops and stand by them. A safe rule of faith:
Support the Pope and the bishops who assist him and obey him.

and all the clergy.

"So ask the Lord of the harvest (especially during holy Mass) to send out laborers into his harvest."

(Mt. 9, 38).

163

Remember our brothers and sisters who have gone to their rest in the hope of rising again; bring them and all the departed into the light of your presence.

Picture of purgatory:
A cloud of unrepented sins prevents the Poor Souls from contemplating the face of Jesus.
Inscription above:
It is a holy and wholesome thought to pray for the dead.
Below: Why do you hide your face?

164

Sancta et Salubris est Cogitatio · Pro Defunctis eXorare

Cur faciem tuam abfcondis?

165

Have mercy on us all; make us worthy to share eternal life with Mary, the virgin mother of God

In the order of grace, Mary's Motherhood continues unceasingly. From her *Fiat* at the Annunciation to which she still clung to under the cross, on to the final completion of all the elect into eternal life.

with the apostles, and with all the saints who have done your will throughout the ages.

May we praise you in union with them, and give you glory through your Son, Jesus Christ.

The Church's dimension is not only concerned with this world, but also the next. Through many of her members she has already attained that completion in Heaven. The pilgrims on this earth have yet to reach this goal on their earthly pilgrimage.

Through him, with him, in him,
in the unity of the Holy Spirit,
all glory and honor is yours,
almighty Father,
for ever and ever.
Amen.

Through the Divine Savior, now present here at the altar, the most incomprehensible event takes place.

Let us pray with confidence to
the Father in the words our
Savior gave us:

Our Father, who art in heaven,
hallowed be thy name;
thy kingdom come;
thy will be done on earth
as it is in heaven.

The Our Father is the crown of all prayers.
It is the recurring and dominant theme and
the corner stone of all Christian devotion.

Give us this day our daily bread;
and forgive us our trespasses
as we forgive those
who trespass against us;
and lead us not into
temptation,
but deliver us from evil.

The Our Father is directed to heaven millions of times as an intercessory prayer and never in vain. But how often, or seldom, is this prayer of petition followed by a prayer of thanksgiving?

174

Deliver us, Lord, from every evil, and grant us peace in our day. In your mercy keep us free from sin and protect us from all anxiety as we wait in joyful hope for the coming of our Savior, Jesus Christ

For the kingdom, the power, and the glory are yours, now and for ever.

The picture:
Elizabeth, who served the Lord in the poor, could wait for his coming with confidence.

Lord Jesus Christ,
you said to your apostles:
I leave you peace,
my peace I give you.
Look not on our sins,
but on the faith of your Church,
and grant us the peace and unity
of your kingdom where you live
for ever and ever. Amen

The peace of the Lord be with
you always.

And also with you.

Lamb of God,
you take away the sins of
the world:
have mercy on us.

Lamb of God,
you take away the sins of
the world:
have mercy on us.

Lamb of God,
you take away the sins of
the world:
grant us peace.

How greatly Jesus was burdened by our
sins!

(cf. 1 Peter, 2, 24)

This is the Lamb of God who takes away the sins of the world. Happy are those who are called to his supper.

Isaiah was the first who compared the Redeemer with a meek sacrificial lamb. John the Baptist took up this call. There is no salvation without Jesus. All blessings flow from him.

Lord, I am not worthy to receive you, but only say the word and I shall be healed.

Referring to the Centurion from Capernaum, Jesus turns to his disciples, points to the Centurion and says: "I have not found such faith in all of Israel."

185

Happy are those who are called to the wedding banquet of the Lamb.

Our picture:
The angel points out the Lamb of God to John and the heavenly Jerusalem, which is open to all nations and the four corners of the earth. Happy are those who are called to his eternal banquet. Holy Communion on earth is but the first step. Blessed indeed are those who may enter the heavenly Jerusalem.

Prayer after Communion

Let us pray:

Lord Jesus Christ,
let the reception of your body
and blood be a foretaste for us of
the glory to come.
You satisfy us in the eternal life
with the full enjoyment of your
glory.
You who live and reign for ever
and ever. Amen

A century will progress or regress in the
same measure as it venerates the Blessed
Sacrament.

The Lord be with you.
And also with you.
May almighty God bless you,
the Father, and the Son,
and the Holy Spirit.
Amen.

Our picture:
The ancestor of Christ, Jacob, blesses his son Joseph and his grandchildren. The blessing of Christ endures from generation to generation and lasts through all ages.

Go in the peace of Christ.

Thanks be to God.

It is you who brighten our path.
You are the way,
the truth and the life.

Eucharistic Prayer I

The Roman Canon

We come to you, Father,
with praise and thanksgiving,
through Jesus Christ your Son.
Through him we ask you to accept and bless these gifts we offer to you in sacrifice.

Everything we have comes from God. We owe him everything. The best expression of our total belonging to God is sacrifice. But only through Christ can we offer God a worthy sacrifice, for he is the Son of God and the Son of man.

We offer them for your holy catholic Church, watch over it, Lord, and guide it; grant it peace and unity throughout the world. We offer them for N. our Pope,

The sacrifice of Christ benefits the whole Church led by the Pope and the bishops. "As the Father has sent me, so I send you. Whoever hears you, hears me."

for N. our bishop, and for all who hold and teach the catholic faith that comes to us from the apostles.

Obey your superiors and be subject to them, because they watch over your souls and have to give an accounting.

Remember, Lord, your people, especially those for whom we now pray, N. and N.
Remember all of us gathered here before you.
You know how firmly we believe in you and dedicate ourselves to you.

If you pray only for yourself, you pray alone. If, however, you pray for all, all pray for you.

(St. Ambrose)

203

We offer you this sacrifice of praise for ourselves and those who are dear to us.

We pray to you, our living and true God, for our well-being and redemption.

His love makes us a new people, heirs of the New Covenant and singers of new hymns. Through Christ we received the greatest and most precious covenant, the participation in His divine nature.

In union with the whole Church we honor Mary, the ever-virgin mother of Jesus Christ our Lord and God. We honor Joseph, her husband,

May Joseph and Mary intercede for us before God and be an example for our families.

the apostles and martyrs
Peter and Paul, Andrew, James,
John, Thomas, James, Philip,
Bartholomew, Matthew, Simon
and Jude;

We are built upon the foundation of the
Apostles. The corner stone is Christ. With
this awareness, we also celebrate the Eucharist in union with the Apostles. Jesus
celebrated Eucharist for the first time with
the Apostles.

we honor Linus, Cletus, Clement, Sixtus, Cornelius, Cyprian, Lawrence,

Following the names of the Apostles the names of five holy Popes are mentioned. Almost all of them are immediate successors to Peter, and then Bishop Cyprian and the Deacon Lawrence.
Our picture: The holy Pope Sixtus

Chrysogonus, John and Paul, Cosmas and Damian and all the saints.
May their merits and prayers gain us your constant help and protection.

Of the great assembly of lay intercessors only five are mentioned; lastly the doctors Cosmas and Damian. They encourage us to pray for the sick. Let us also pray for all whose life is endangered through no fault of their own (victims of accidents, assassinations, abortion, or euthanasia)! Let us pray for the terminally ill and the dying!

Father, accept this offering from your whole family.
Grant us your peace in this life, save us from final damnation, and count us among those you have chosen.

"I will receive you and will be a father to you and you will be my sons and daughters" says the Lord God, the Almighty.

Bless and approve our offering:
make it acceptable to you,
an offering in spirit and in truth.
Let it become for us the body
and blood of Jesus Christ,
your only Son, our Lord.

God the Father bestowed upon us all spiritual blessings through Jesus Christ.

The day before he suffered he took bread in his sacred hands and looking up to heaven, to you, his almighty Father, he gave you thanks and praise. He broke the bread, gave it to his disciples, and said:
Take this, all of you, and eat it: this is my body which will be given up for you.

Is not the bread that we break a participation in the body of Christ?

When supper was ended, he took the cup. Again he gave you thanks and praise, gave the cup to his disciples, and said:

Take this, all of you, and drink from it: this is the cup of my blood, the blood of the new and everlasting covenant. It will be shed for you and for all so that sins may be forgiven.

Is the chalice of salvation over which we speak a blessing not a participation in the blood of Christ?

Do this in memory of me.

Christ bestowed the power to transform bread and wine, as well as the power to forgive sins only to his Apostles, and not upon the whole Church. Consequently the Apostles passed on this power to selected persons. "They (Paul and Barnabas) appointed presbyters in each church and, with prayer and fasting, commended them to the Lord in whom they had put their faith." (Acts 14, 23)

Let us proclaim the mystery
of faith:

Dying you destroyed our death,

Every time, then, you eat this bread and
drink this cup, you proclaim the death of
the Lord until he comes!

(1 Cor. 11, 26)

224

**rising you restored our life.
Lord Jesus, come in glory.**

We know that Christ, after his resurrection,
dies no more. Look upon yourselves as dead
to sin but alive to God through Jesus
Christ.

(cf. Rom. 6, 9–11)

226

Father, we celebrate the memory of Christ, your Son. We, your people and your ministers, recall his passion,

His sacrifice brings salvation to all, the just and the unjust.

his resurrection from the dead, and his ascension into glory;

"If then you were raised with Christ, seek what is above, where Christ is seated at the right hand of God. Think of what is above, not of what is on earth. For you have died, and your life is hidden with Christ in God. When Christ, your life, appears then you too will appear with him in glory."

(Col. 3, 1–4)

230

and from the many gifts you have given us we offer to you, God of glory and majesty, this holy and perfect sacrifice: the bread of life and the cup of eternal salvation.

Christ, flame of eternal love, kindle in our hearts the fire of your love, so that we may love you above all and our brothers and sister for the love of you.

Look with favor on these offerings and accept them as once you accepted the gifts of your servant Abel, the sacrifice of Abraham, our father in faith, and the bread and wine offered by your priest Melchisedech.

The many sacrifices ever offered by humankind find their consummation in the sacrifice of the new covenant.

235

Almighty God,
we pray that your angel may
take this sacrifice to your altar in
heaven.

Who of the faithful could doubt that at the
hour the Eucharist is offered, heaven opens
up; and that the choirs of angels participate
in this mystery of Jesus Christ.

(Pope Gregory the Great)

Then, as we receive from this altar the sacred body and blood of your Son, let us be filled with every grace and blessing.

Of this abundance of grace it can truly be said: "Neither the first nor the last who attempted to do so can fathom it."
Our picture: The stream of grace descending upon the earth.

Remember, Lord, those who have died and have gone before us marked with the sign of faith, especially those for whom we now pray, N. and N.

May our departed loved ones reach eternal bliss through the limitless mercy of God, the atoning sacrifice of Christ, through the intercession of the Blessed Mother and all the saints.

May these, and all who sleep in Christ, find in your presence light, happiness, and peace.

Remembering the departed during the celebration of the Divine Mysteries is not fruitless. We intercede for them with the Lamb of God who takes away the sins of the world.

(St. Chrysostom)

For ourselves, too, we ask some share in the fellowship of your apostles and martyrs, with John the Baptist, Stephen, Matthias, Barnabas (Ignatius, Alexander, Marcellinus, Peter,

The Holy Mass is the bridge uniting the Pilgrim Church on earth with the Suffering Church in Purgatory and the Church Triumphant in Heaven.

Felicity, Perpetua, Agatha, Lucy, Agnes, Cecilia, Anastasia) and all the saints.

Though we are sinners, we trust in your mercy and love. Do not consider what we truly deserve, but grant us your forgiveness. Through Christ, our Lord.

We implore the holy women Perpetua and Felicity for the grace for happy and lasting marriages. We ask the radiant and youthful saints Agatha, Agnes, Cecilia and Maria Goretti for the grace of purity for our young men and women. We call upon them for vocations to the priestly and religious life, for Sisters to staff our schools and hospitals, and for priests to lead our priestless parishes.

247

Through him you give us all these gifts. You fill them with life and goodness, you bless them and make them holy.

There is an enormous potential of love in the Redeemer, Jesus Christ, a love which knows each one and is intent on each one's salvation. The symbol of this love is the pierced heart of the Savior.

Through him, with him, in him,
in the unity of the Holy Spirit,
all glory and honor is yours,
almighty Father,
for ever and ever.
Amen.

It would be wrong to direct our efforts and
deeds to increase our own honor. To you
alone, Lord, be honor and glory.

251

Let us pray with confidence to
the Father in the words our
Savior gave us.

Our Father, who art in heaven,
hallowed be thy name;
thy kingdom come;
thy will be done on earth as it is
in heaven.

When we say the Our Father we use Divine
words. "The Our Father can convert even
an atheist."
Our picture: Jesus points to heaven.

Give us this day our daily bread;
and forgive us our trespasses
as we forgive those
who trespass against us;
and lead us not into temptation,
but deliver us from evil.

When we think of the sacrifice on the cross
we must imitate Jesus' forgiving love.

Our picture:
Jesus points to his Apostles and to us.

255

Deliver us, Lord,
from every evil,
and grant us peace in our day.
In your mercy keep us free from
sin and protect us from all
anxiety as we wait in joyful hope
for the coming of our Savior,
Jesus Christ.

We meet Christ in the poor.
Let us imitate Jesus!

Our picture:
St. Lawrence reaches out to the poor.

257

**For the kingdom,
the power
and the glory are yours,
now and for ever.**

May he rule from sea to sea, and from one end of the earth to the other.

All kings shall pay him homage, all nations shall serve him (whether they want to or not!)

(cf. Ps 72)

Lord Jesus Christ,
you said to your apostles:
I leave you peace,
my peace I give you.
Look not on our sins,
but on the faith of your Church,
and grant us the peace and unity
of your kingdom where you live
for ever and ever.
The peace of the Lord be with
you always.
And also with you.

Lamb of God, you take away the sins of the world:
have mercy on us.

Lamb of God, you take away the sins of the world:
have mercy on us.

Lamb of God, you take away the sins of the world:
grant us peace.

Jesus wiped out the letter of indictment against us by nailing it to the cross.

This is the Lamb of God who takes away the sins of the world. Happy are those who are called to his supper.

We approach holy communion as poor and sinful human beings. We are burdened by the power of evil. St. John, however, tells us: do not look upon yourselves, look upon the Lamb of God. Leave all despondency behind. Cooperate with God's grace. The Lamb will reign and so will those who are faithful to him.

Lord, I am not worthy to receive you, but only say the word and I shall be healed.

The Church memorialized the humble Centurion of Caparnaum for all times by using his words at every communion.

I am with you,
even to the ends of the world.

Christ is present on the altar not only at the time of Communion, but from the moment of consecration and for as long as the sacred species are present.

Next to receiving Holy Communion, no other devotion is more pleasing to God than frequent visits to the churches in whose tabernacles He is present.

Prayer after Communion

Let us pray.

Lord God, we worship you,
a Trinity of Persons,
one eternal God.
May our faith and the sacrament
we receive bring us health of
mind and body.
We ask this through Christ our
Lord.

The greater the grace is, which Jesus bestows upon us by his continuous presence
in the holy Eucharist, the greater also is our
obligation to honor this sublime sacrament.

The Lord be with you.
And also with you.
May almighty God bless you,
the Father, and the Son, and the
Holy Spirit.
Go in peace to love and serve the
Lord.
Thanks be to God.

How frequently is it possible for me to attend Holy Mass? Daily, perhaps?
In retirement? Or, may be already today?

Eucharistic Prayer III

Father, you are holy indeed,
and all creation rightly
gives you praise.
All life, all holiness comes from
you through your Son,
Jesus Christ our Lord,
by the working
of the Holy Spirit.

The triune God wants to be honored
through a united Christian Community.

From age to age you gather a people to yourself, so that from east to west a perfect offering may be made to the glory of your name.

From the rising of the sun to its setting, my name is great among the nations, and a perfect offering is made in my name in every place.

And so, Father, we bring you these gifts.
We ask you to make them holy by the power of Your spirit,
that they may become the body and blood of your Son,
our Lord Jesus Christ,
at whose command we celebrate this eucharist.

Creation! Stand in awe! Your Creator is coming, your Redeemer, o humankind.

On the night he was betrayed,
he took bread and gave you
thanks and praise.
He broke the bread,
gave it to his disciples, and said:
Take this, all of you, and eat it:
this is my body which will be
given up for you.

It was not by accident but by divine prov-
idence that God's sacrificing love became
evident in the most wonderful and soul-
searching manner during this night, the
night of betrayal.

When supper was ended,
he took the cup.
Again he gave you thanks
and praise, gave the cup to his
disciples, and said:
Take this, all of you
and drink from it:
this is the cup of my blood,
the blood of the new and
everlasting covenant.
It will be shed for you and for all
so that sins may be forgiven.

To respond to such a love, to his giving the last drop of his blood for us, should be a matter of course. We can do this, for example, through conscientious and frequent participation in the Holy Eucharist, especially on Sundays and Holy Days.

Do this in memory of me.

The Holy Sacrifice of the Mass can be validly celebrated in every place by the one to whom the power was passed on in uninterrupted succession. Thus every place where a duly ordained bishop or priest celebrates the Eucharist becomes the Place of the Last Supper.

Let us proclaim the mystery of faith:
When we eat this bread
and drink this cup,
we proclaim your death,
Lord Jesus,
until you come in glory.

Jesus is truly present in the form of bread and wine. He wanted to be present under both these species, so different from each other. The separation of his body and blood on the wood of the cross is clearly illustrated.

Father, calling to mind the death your Son endured for our salvation, his glorious resurrection and ascension into heaven, and ready to greet him when he comes again, we offer you in thanksgiving this holy and living sacrifice.

If Jesus had not risen from the dead, we would still be living in our sins.

Look with favor on your
Church's offering,
and see the Victim whose death
has reconciled us to yourself.

Humankind, by itself, cannot effect its salvation. Salvation was accomplished by the Lamb of God when he sacrificed his own life.

Grant that we,
who are nourished by his body
and blood,
may be filled with his
Holy Spirit,
and become one body,
one spirit in Christ.

Miraculous consequence of holy communion! At this very moment we are united with Christ and through Christ with the most holy Trinity. Through Christ, the head, we are also united in grace with the mystical body of the whole Church.

May he make us an everlasting gift to you and enable us to share in the inheritance of your saints, with Mary, the virgin mother of God;

How close we now are to the saints, especially the Blessed Mother! She suffered with Jesus more than anyone else and was also glorified more than anyone else. She's the First Fruit of salvation and a source of consolation to the Pilgrim Church.

**with the apostles,
the martyrs,
(Saint N. – the saint of the day
or the patron saint)**

Jesus promised his Apostles: You who have followed me will also sit on twelve thrones when the Son of Man enters into His glory. When celebrating the Holy Eucharist, we offer that sacrifice from which all martyrdom took its source.

**and all your saints,
on whose constant intercession
we rely for help.**

We pray to the Holy Trinity for mercy. We pray to the saints so that they will intercede for us before God. It is a good practice to read the life of the saints in the evening in preparation for the next day.

Lord, may this sacrifice, which has made our peace with you, advance the peace and salvation of all the world.

Through the Cross Jesus redeemed the whole world. The salvation from all evil occurs when God calls: "Enter into the joy of your Lord!"
Our picture: The Church on its journey to God through time.

Strengthen in faith and love
your pilgrim Church on earth;

Examples of faith and love:

St. Bernadette Soubirou
1844–1879

St. Theresa of the Child Jesus
1873–1897

Abbess Caritas Pirckheimer
1467–1532

Blessed Stilla of Abenberg
12th century.

your servant, Pope N.,
our bishop N.,
and all the bishops,
with the clergy and the
entire people your Son
has gained for us.

Our picture:
Christ hands the key of heaven to the first
Pope. The Church repels the attacks of Satan with the sign of the cross.

Father, hear the prayers of the family you have gathered here before you. In mercy and love unite all your children wherever they may be.

Our picture:
Paul points to the inscription: "To the unknown God" and says: "The one you venerate, without knowing him, is the one I announce to you: the Son of God who died for us and rose from the grave."

G.B.Göz. Inv. & Pinx.

Welcome into your kingdom
our departed brothers
and sisters,
and all who have left this world
in your friendship.

A soul still burdened by minor offenses would find it unacceptable to appear in the full radiance of heaven. It has but one desire: to purify itself.

We hope to enjoy for ever
the vision of your glory,

Christianity is not a club for friends of an-
tiquity, but the challenge of today and the
hope for the future.

**through Christ our Lord,
from whom all good things
come.**

The Divinity without the Humanity is no
intercessor. The Humanity without the Divinity is no intercessor. The only intercessor between God and Man is Jesus
Christ. Jesus has come that we may have
life and have it to the full. How much grat-
itude we owe him for that!

Through him, with him, in him,
in the unity of the Holy Spirit,
all glory and honor is yours,
almighty Father,
for ever and ever.
Amen.

O Lord, my God, you are my only hope.
Listen to my prayer that I may not weaken
in my search for you. I want to search for
your countenance with ever greater ardor
and fervor.

Let us pray . . .

Our Father, who art in heaven, hallowed by thy name; thy kingdom come; thy will be done on earth as it is in heaven.

God, who prefers to be loved rather than feared, would much rather be called Father than Lord.
You have not received the spirit that calls you to be slaves, but rather the spirit that calls you to be sons and daughters, the spirit in which we cry out: Abba, Father!

Give us this day our daily bread;
and forgive us our trespasses
as we forgive those
who trespass against us;
and lead us not into temptation,
but deliver us from evil.

St. Cyprian: "Jesus did not teach us to pray *my* daily bread, but *our* daily bread," the bread for all nations, irrespective of race or color!

Would The Lord's prayer, which begins with the invocation to our common father, make any sense if we are not willing to share with the hungry?

Deliver us, Lord,
from every evil,
and grant us peace in our day.
In your mercy keep us free from
sin and protect us from all
anxiety as we wait in joyful hope
for the coming of our Savior,
Jesus Christ.

Our picture:
Christ with Martha and Mary:
You have taken me into your house. I lead
you into the house of my heavenly Father.

For the kingdom,
the power,
and the glory are yours,
now and for ever.

The wounds and blood of Christ reveal the
enormous guilt of humanity, but even more
the victorious mercy of God.

DOMINE IN TE SPERAVI
NON CONFVNDAR IN
AETERNVM QVIA REDEMISTI
ME DEVS VERITATIS

Lord Jesus Christ, you said to your apostles:
I leave you peace, my peace I give you. Look not on our sins, but on the faith of your Church, and grant us the peace and unity of your kingdom where you live for ever and ever. Amen
The peace of the Lord be with you always.
And also with you.

Komet und bela=
stu Mir, den seid
alle, die, Ich will
ihr müh euch er
selig.
quicken.

Herz Jesu
Heil aller die
auf dich hoffen
erbarme dich
unser!

Lamb of God, you take
away the sins of the world:
have mercy on us.

Lamb of God, you take
away the sins of the world:
have mercy on us.

Lamb of God, you take
away the sins of the world:
Grant us peace.

You are the atoning sacrifice for our sins,
but not only for our sins, but for the sins of
the whole world.
You yourself are the victim and sacrificial
priest, the true lamb, who takes away the
sins of the world.

329

This is the Lamb of God
who takes away
the sins of the world.

The sacrifice on the cross is an absolute sacrifice. The Eucharist is a relative sacrifice, since it is in direct relationship to the sacrifice on the cross.

The Council of Trent teaches: Christ left to his Church a visible sacrifice in the bloody sacrifice which has taken place on the cross and is now sacramentally represented as his memorial to the ends of the world and as a saving force for the forgiveness of sins.

Lord, I am not worthy
to receive you,
but only say the word
and I shall be healed.

Based on our own righteousness we are
never worthy. Even if we were, we would
still be unworthy without appropriate hu-
mility.

The Word became flesh;
we have seen his glory.

Jesus tells me:
"I stand before the door and knock.
Whoever hears my voice and opens the
door, I will enter there and I will eat a meal
with them and they with me."

Prayer after Communion

Let us pray.

Lord,
in this sacrament we receive
the promise of salvation;
make us grow in faith and love
to celebrate the coming of
Christ our Savior,
who is Lord for ever and ever.
Amen.

How diligently we must strive for godliness
and a change of heart. Thus we await and
long for the coming of Jesus.

The Lord be with you.
And also with you.

God is our refuge and strength, our glorious solace in affliction.
Let us not be afraid even if the earth quakes and the mountains plunge into the depth of the sea, when the waters foam and the mountains tremble at his might.

May almighty God bless you,
the Father,
and the Son,
and the Holy Spirit.
Amen.

Beloved Mother Mary Immaculate, all you
angels and saints in the heavens, all creatures on the earth I implore you:
Love, adore and praise the Father, the Son
and the Holy Spirit in my behalf.
Praise the Trinity for all graces and blessings of the past, the present and future.
The triune God has thought of us from the
beginning of time. Offer thanks with me
for this infinite love.

341

**The Mass is ended, go in peace.
Thanks be to God.**

The way to heaven is not a wide and comfortable road, but narrow and steep.
Yet heaven is worth more than anything on earth.

342

Eucharistic Prayer IV

Father in heaven, it is right that we should give you thanks and glory: you are the one God, living and true.
Through all eternity you live in unapproachable light.

Everyone of his attributes, his holiness, eternity and love give us reason to rejoice, praise and offer thanks.

Source of life and goodness,
you have created all things,
to fill your creatures with every
blessing and lead all men to the
joyful vision of your light.

Whoever is not enlightened by such a
splendor of creatures is blind. Whoever
does not perceive the origin of creation is a
fool.

(St. Bonaventure)

Countless hosts of angels stand before you to do your will; they look upon your splendor and praise you, night and day.

O God, your will be done; in heaven by the angels, and on earth by us human beings.

United with them, and in the name of every creature under heaven, we too praise your glory and sing:

No matter what one might think or whatever one might say: God is greater! No language is adequate to pronounce his name.

(St. Thomas Aquinas)

352

353

Holy, holy, holy
Lord, God of power and might,
heaven and earth are full
of your glory.
Hosanna in the highest.
Blessed is he who comes in the
name of the Lord.
Hosanna in the highest.

Do not forget the purpose of the miraculous creation. Admire, venerate and see in it the all-wise creator. It is of little purpose to admire nature if it does not lead us to God.

Father, we acknowledge your greatness: all your actions show your wisdom and love.

You created the universe and ordered everything by size, number and weight. You love everything you created. You despise nothing you have made.

You also love me.

You formed man in your own likeness and set him over the whole world to serve you, his creator, and to rule over all creatures.

How beautiful it would be on earth if men and women, your creatures, would serve you alone, their creator.

Even when he disobeyed you and lost your friendship you did not abandon him to the power of death, but helped all men to seek and find you.

It would have been of little value to all human beings if we had been created but not redeemed.

(cf. Exultet)

Again and again you offered a covenant to man, and through the prophets taught him to hope for salvation.

Isaiah 61, 1: "The spirit of the Lord God is upon me, because the Lord has anointed me. He has sent me . . ."

The names of the four major prophets are: Ezekiel, Daniel, Isaiah and Jeremiah. The names of the twelve minor prophets are: Hosea, Joel, Amos, Obadiah, Jonah, Micah, Nahum, Habakkuk, Zephaniah, Haggai, Zechariah and Malachi.

Lucæ 4.
Der Geist des Herren
ist über mir, und der
Herr hat mich gesandt.

Father, you so loved the world that in the fullness of time you sent your only Son to be our Savior.

How far-reaching was your paternal love? In order to redeem the servant, you gave your son. He came to heal the sick, the poor, the sinners, for the redemption of the prodigal son, to heal Lazarus, and to save a world condemned to death.

He was conceived through the power of the Holy Spirit, and born of the Virgin Mary, a man like us in all things but sin.

Jesus could not endure that death would prevail over us. Therefore he became man - human like us - but in a most miraculous manner through the Blessed Virgin Mary.

To the poor he proclaimed the good news of salvation,
to prisoners, freedom, and to those in sorrow, joy.

Time and again, I read in the Bible how good the Lord has been to us, without cunning or deceit; how readily he showed mercy to all the sick and called the lowly and the poor his brothers and sisters.

In fulfillment of your will he gave himself up to death:

The Cross of Christ gives everything its true value, all fortunes, advantages, honors, pleasures, all lust of the flesh and eyes, as well as the pride of life. The Cross of Christ gives meaning to afflictions, temptations and sufferings of this life.

**but by rising from the dead,
he destroyed death and restored
life.**

Jesus has returned from death, or better:
He has gone beyond death.
His Resurrection – and therefore ours as
well – is not one among the many but a beginning of the "now" without end.

And that we might live no longer for ourselves but for him,

St. Paul, as did John the Baptist before him, said: "Jesus must increase, I must decrease. I am not even worthy to untie the straps of his sandals."

he sent the Holy Spirit from you, Father, as his first gift to those who believe,

A mere personality cult bogs us down in pure humanitarianism. True progress in the Church as well as in the individual soul is only possible through the intervention of the Holy Spirit.

to complete his work on earth and bring us the fullness of grace.

We cannot enter a catholic church without being reminded of the enormous gifts the Holy Spirit has bestowed upon us. What message is conveyed to us by the baptismal font, the confessional, the lectern, and the tabernacle? Do not let us forget that we live by the graces of the Holy Spirit.

378

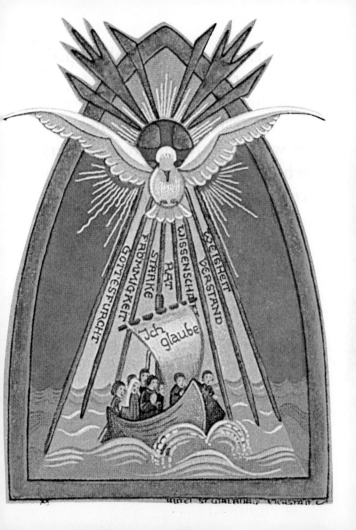

Father, may this Holy Spirit sanctify these offerings.
Let them become the body and blood of Jesus Christ our Lord as we celebrate the great mystery which he left us as an everlasting covenant.

An arch of uninterrupted celebration of the Eucharist spans the Last Supper to the day of the end of the world. How fortunate we are to have the undeserved privilege to share in it!

Do we treasure this grace?

Do we make the best possible use of it?

He always loved those who were his own in the world.

When the time came for him to be glorified by you, his heavenly Father, he showed the depth of his love.

While they were at supper, he took bread, said the blessing, broke the bread and gave it to his disciples, saying:

Take this, all of you, and eat it: this is my body which will be given up for you.

Could Jesus have done any more? John responds "Since he loved his own, he loved them to the end." Here the highest unites with the lowest, the earthly is one with the heavenly.

In the same way, he took the cup, filled with wine.

He gave you thanks, and giving the cup to his disciples, said:

Take this, all of you, and drink from it: this is the cup of my blood, the blood of the new and everlasting covenant. It will be shed for you and for all so that sins may be forgiven.

Our picture:
The miracle at the wedding at Cana.
At the last supper, in the new and everlasting covenant, an even greater miracle is wrought between the divine groom and his bride, the Church.

Do this in memory of me.

In order that the fullness of divine power be validly handed down, the Church required that every new bishop be ordained by three bishops.

(Council of Nissa 325)

Even after their separation from Rome (1054), the Orthodox Church continued to consecrate their bishops in the same manner. Their ordination of bishops and priests is valid.

Our picture:
The ordination of St. Willibald by Bishop St. Boniface and two additional bishops.

Let us proclaim
the mystery of faith:

All creatures of the earth should be terrified by the crucifixion. The seriousness of the redemption through the bloody sacrifice of the cross must not be downplayed. Otherwise the Holy Eucharist would be degraded to merely a social banquet. The cross must be the focal point.

388

Lord, by your cross and resurrection you have set us free. You are the Savior of the world.

How quickly the exploits of the world are relegated to history. The fact of Jesus' resurrection, however, is always current and called to mind at every holy Mass. For us mortals it is a ray of light, an objective for eternal life, and a never ending future.

Father, we now celebrate this
memorial of our redemption.
We recall Christ's deaths,

Paul, however, also tells us: Mindful of
God's mercy, I admonish you, my brothers
and sisters, to offer yourself as a living and
holy sacrifice, pleasing to God. For you this
is the true and proper worship. We should
consider ourselves as dead to sin, but alive
in Christ Jesus.

his descent among the dead, his resurrection, and his ascension to your right hand; and, looking forward to his coming in glory,

The work of redemption encompasses all past and future generations.

Our picture:
He "descended" to those earlier dead, Adam and Eve, David, Joseph . . .

we offer you his body and blood, the acceptable sacrifice which brings salvation to the whole world.

It is written early in scripture: "Sacrifice you did not desire, but you have given me a body."
Every eucharistic celebration recalls Christ's atoning sacrifice. Jesus has shed his blood for the forgiveness of sins!

Lord, look upon this sacrifice which you have given to your Church; and by your Holy Spirit, gather all who share this one bread and one cup into the one body of Christ, a living sacrifice of praise.

The effects of a good holy Communion are: union with Christ the head, union with the mystical body of Christ and association with the self-sacrificing Christ.

Lord, remember those for whom we offer this sacrifice, especially N., our Pope, N., our bishop, and bishops and clergy everywhere.

Conscious of the presence of Jesus' sacrifice on the cross in the celebration of the Eucharist, St. Francis Borgia placed into the wound of the right hand of Jesus, the Pope and all bishops and priests, and into the wound of the left hand all secular authority.

Remember those who take part in this offering, those here present and all your people, and all who seek you with a sincere heart.

Into the wound of the right foot St. Francis of Borgia placed all religious. Into the wound of the left foot he placed all his relatives, friends and benefactors. Into the wound of the side, he put himself and all of his tasks and intentions. No one was forgotten. When we participate in the sacrifice of Christ who gave himself for the salvation of all mankind, then our heart, too, should be open for the intentions of all our brothers and sisters.

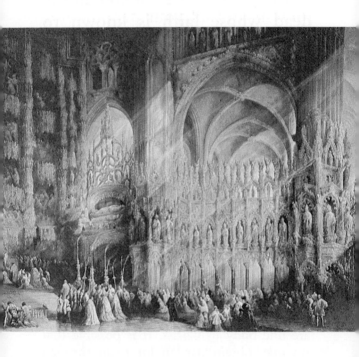

Remember those who have died in the peace of Christ and all the dead whose faith is known to you alone.

St. Francis Borgia also lingered at the prayer for the dead. He placed into the wounds of Jesus all for whom the holy Mass was offered, and then all religious vocations, relatives, friends and benefactors and finally all the souls who are most estranged from God and those that are closest to God.

If Job's sacrifice was an atonement for his children, how can we comfort them? We are one body in Christ. It is possible that we may obtain pardon for them through prayer and sacrifice.

404

Father, in your mercy grant also to us, your children, to enter into our heavenly inheritance in the company of the Virgin Mary, the Mother of God

The first Christians tarried daily in the temple, united in prayer. They broke the Eucharistic bread at home and took their meal with joy and in the simplicity of their heart. The Blessed Mother was one of these first Christians and for us a wonderful model for holy communion.

and your apostles

When the Apostles and Martyrs could pray for others at a time when they were beset by trials, how much more can they do so now having attained victory, triumph and the crown. Our picture shows the Apostle who, at the time of the very first Eucharist, rested on the bosom of the Lord. It is he who recorded for us the high priestly prayer.

and saints.

Our picture:
The blessing of Christ's sacrifice on the cross which is represented in the Eucharist (top left), and the effects of which are shown in the stigmata of St. Francis of Assisi (top right) are of benefit to the saints in heaven (Mary, the Apostles, holy men and women), the praying faithful on earth (represented by the patrons of the artist), and the Holy Souls in Purgatory.

Then, in your kingdom, freed from the corruption of sin and death, we shall sing your glory with every creature through Christ our Lord, through whom you give us everything that is good.

Thus will it be on the day that has no end. We shall see God and love Him, praise and give Him thanks. We will be with Him, and remain with Him. Yes, thus will it be on the final day without end.

(St. Augustine)

Through him, with him, in him,
in the unity of the Holy Spirit,
all glory and honor is yours,
almighty Father,
for ever and ever. Amen

In the heart of Jesus glows the noblest love
that ever radiated from a human heart.
This heart, as a focal point, is even united
in the infinite love of the triune God. You
too should love the Lord your God above
all else, and your neighbor as yourself! You
glorify God mostly through love.

Our picture:
The picture of the Sacred Heart in the University church of Innsbruck.

Our Father,
who art in heaven
hallowed be thy name;
thy kingdom come;
thy will be done on earth
as it is in heaven.

He who fashioned the eye,
should he not see?

(Ps. 94, 9.)

The eye of the Lord rests upon all who revere Him and long for his goodness. His paternal eye encompasses the whole world. We may even dare to pray: "Guard us as the apple of your eye!"

416

Give us this day our daily bread;
and forgive us our trespasses
as we forgive those
who trespass against us;
and lead us not into temptations
but deliver us from evil.

He who fashioned the ear,
should he not hear? (Ps. 94,9)

Where is the father who gives his son a stone when he asks for bread? Now that you who are evil, know how to give good things to your children, how much more will your heavenly Father give the Holy Spirit to those who ask for it! Not only does he give earthly bread, but bread from heaven to all those who love him.

Deliver us, Lord, from every evil, and grant us peace in our day. In your mercy keep us free from sin and protect us from all anxiety as we wait in joyful hope for the coming of our Savior, Jesus Christ.

For the kingdom, the power, and the glory are yours, now and for ever.

Only too well are we, the fallen children of Adam, aware of our shortcomings and weaknesses. We also know that if we humbly acknowledge our weaknesses, we are strong through Christ, our Redeemer.

Lord Jesus Christ,
you said to your apostles:
I leave you peace,
my peace I give you.
Look not on our sins, but on the faith of your Church, and grant us the peace and unity of your kingdom where you live for ever and ever. Amen
The peace of the Lord be with you always.
And also with you.

Our Risen Lord offered the kiss of peace twice to the disciples who failed him. Jesus' example can best help us overcome the big and small difficulties.

Lamb of God, you take
away the sins of the world:
have mercy on us.
Lamb of God, you take
away the sins of the world:
have mercy on us.
Lamb of God, you take
away the sins of the world:
Grant us peace.

Holy Communion, which we are happy to
say is received more frequently today, would
be of still greater benefit if it were ac-
companied by the regular reception of the
sacrament of reconciliation. St. Leonardo of
Porto Maurizio, who was the confessor of the
brilliant Pope Benedict XIV, wrote: "Whoever commits himself to a weekly Confession
and Communion can be certain that he is on
the right way to heaven."

This is the Lamb of God,
who takes away
the sins of the world.
Happy are those
who are called to his supper.

Everyone, hierarchy and laity, are called to be holy according to the word of the Apostle: "This is the will of God; your sanctification."

Pray to God at every holy Mass that he makes a great saint of you! Do you think, perhaps, that this is asking too much? No, this is not asking too much!

Lord, I am not worthy to receive you, but only say the word and I shall be healed.

The Holy Eucharist is not only the life of every Christian, it is also the life of every nation. The sun of the holy Eucharist must rise to dispel the forces of darkness and to melt the ice that covers many a soul. Let us submit to the healing influence of the Eucharistic sun, and the face of the earth will be renewed.

Our God appeared on earth as one among us.

My heart expands and rejoices in the Lord. The same Jesus who came down from heaven by Mary's consent is given to us truly, essentially and substantially in the holy Eucharist. The annunciation by Veit Stoss and the tabernacle by Adam Kraft, depicted on the right, remind us of this mystery.

Prayer after Communion

Lord Jesus Christ,
you give us your body and blood in the eucharist as a sign that even now we share your life.
May we come to possess it completely in the kingdom where you live for ever and ever.

May I be saturated by our Lord Jesus Christ as the cloth is by dye or the air by light! Christ wants to pass on his sacrificing love to the world through us.

432

May almighty God bless you,
the Father, and the Son,
and the Holy Spirit.

How richly you confer upon us your gifts!
You give us life and sustain it. You give us
sanctifying and remedial grace. You give us
your life. You give us yourself. You want to
give us heaven. Then, too, give us the grace
that we may always be grateful for your
blessing.

The Mass is ended,
go in peace.

Whoever knows the Catholic Church only as an institution, even as the most enduring one, has not grasped the essence of the Church. She is an innermost "Mystery". She is the mystical body of Christ and Christ is her head. She is the Christ who continues to live and work in time and space.

436

Acknowledgements: I wish to thank all public and private authorities both in Germany and abroad for their cooperation. I am specially grateful to all who reduced or completely waived the customary charges because of the religious nature of the publications.

Footnotes and Abbreviations

Herder, Ikonographie der christl. Kunst
Gotteslob
Lektionare des Stundengebets
Dr. Holböck Ferdinand, Das Allerheiligste und die Heiligen: Holböck, A.
Dr. Holböck Ferdinand, Ergriffen vom Dreieinigen Gott: Holböck, E.
Koch Anton, Homilet. Quellenwerk: Koch
Dr. Könn Josef, Die heilige Messe: Könn
Nußbaum, Die neuen Hochgebete
Ott, Handbuch der Dogmatik
Dr. Schnitzler Theodor, Die drei neuen eucharist. Hochgebete: Schnitzler

Seite:

438

120 ▷ 44
124 Karl Adam, Christus unser Bruder
128 Koch
132 und 138 nach Hieronymus
142 Chrysostomus, s. Holböck, A. 52
146 2 Tim 1,6 u. 1 Tim 5,22
148 ▷ 44
152 Gertrud von Le Fort, Hymnen
166 Lumen gentium, Art. 61/62
168 Faulhaber, Zeitrufe
172 Bischof Paul Wilhelm v. Keppler
174 F. W. Faber, Vom Danksagen
180 vgl. 1 Petr. 2,24
182 vgl. Könn 276
188 P. Julian Eymard, s. Holböck, A, 368
200 Hebr. 13,17
204 a) Augustinus b) 2 Petr, 1,4
208 2 Kor 4,6
208 Könn 126
210 Könn 127
212 Könn 127
214 2 Kor 6,18/216 Stundenbuch III (Im Jahreskreis) 691
216 vgl. Eph 1,3
218 und 220 1 Kor 10,16
224 1 Kor 11,26
234 vgl. Gabengebet v. 16.So. im Jahreskreis
236 Gregor d. Große, s. Holböck, A. 59
238 Weisheit 24,28
242 Chrysostomus
246 Abt Dr. Thomas Niggl, Weltenburg
248 Schamoni Wilhelm, Theolog. Rückblick 171
262 Kol 2,14
264 Könn, 277
266 Könn 280
268 Alfons Maria Liguori, s. Holböck, A 322
270 Karl Borromäus, s. Holböck, A 246
276 Ökumen. Erklärung 1981, s. Holböck, E 399
278 Maleachi, 1,11
290 vgl. 1 Kor 15,17
296 vgl. Lumen gentium 8,68

298 a) Mt 19,28 b) Messe vom Do.n.d. 3. Fastensonntag
300 Thomas v. Aquin
308 vgl. Apg. 17,22
310 Keppler, Die Armenseelenpredigt 37
314 Augustinus, siehe Koch 232,3,5
316 Holböck, E 99
318 Lektionar z. Stundenbuch I,3,114 und Rom 8,15
320 Cyprian und Sonnenschein, Notizen zum 12.7.25
328 vgl. 1 Joh 2,2 und vgl. Cyrill v. Alexandrien
330 Ott Ludwig, Grundriß der Dogmatik, 10. Auflage, S. 484
332 Katharina v. Siena, s. Holböck, A 160
334 Offb. 3,20
336 2 Petr. 3,11
338 Ps. 46,2 f
340 Vinzenz Palotti, s. Holböck, E 332
354 vgl. Joh. Kepler, Das Weltgeheimnis, Schlußwort
356 Weisheit 11,20 u. 24
360 vgl. Exultet
364 Exultet und H. Schell
366 Athanasius
368 Luise Hensel
370 Kardinal J.H. Newman
372 Kardinal Josef Ratzinger
378 Schnitzler 117
386 Ott, a.a.O. 546
388 Papst Leo d. Große und Dr. Overath J., „Heiliges Brot" oder Leib
     Christi? S. 23
392 Ro 12,1 und 6,11
396 vgl. Hebr. 1,5f
400-404 vgl. Holböck, A 229 f
406 vgl. Holböck, A 426
412 Augustinus, s. Gotteslob, Eichstätt 1952, Seite 984
416 Ps. 94,9; Ps. 33,18; 2 Chr. 16,9; Ps. 17,8
418 Ps. 94,9; Lk 11,11; Joh 6,32
420 vgl. Könn 260
424 Leonhard von Porto Maurizio, s. Holböck, A 316
426 a) Dogmat. Konstitution über die Kirche V,39
     b) Leonh. v. Porto Maurizio, s. Holböck, A 315
428 P. Julian Eymard, s. Holböck, A 368
432 Bernhardin v. Siena

440

Notes on the Illustrations

Abkürzungen: F bedeutet Fotograf, St = Standort. ▷ = Hinweis auf frühere Seite

1. Äußerer Umschlag: Max Gattinger, Rokokogitter, 1743 Kloster-kirche Ebrach
   Foto Hermann Mayer, 8501 Rückersdorf, Hohe Linde 14
2. Inneres Titelblatt: Abteikirche Ottobeuren 1737—1766
   Foto Dr. Hans Hebeisen, Wiesbaden, Wilhelmstr. 52 E/ 368

442

445

446

447

448